CHARM BRACELET STUDIO

BY THE EDITORS OF KLUTZ

KLUTZ®

KLUTZ® creates activity books and other great stuff for kids ages 3 to 103. We began our corporate life in 1977 in a garage we shared with a Chevrolet Impala. Although we've outgrown that first office, Klutz galactic headquarters is still staffed entirely by real human beings. For those of you who collect mission statements, here's ours:

· CREATE WONDERFUL THINGS · BE GOOD · HAVE FUN

WRITE US

We would love to hear your comments regarding this or any of our books.

KLUTZ®
568 Broadway, Suite 503
New York, NY 10012
thefolks@klutz.com

Finishing gloss manufactured in USA. Box, stickers, and paint manufactured in China. All other parts, Taiwan. 85

Published by Klutz, a subsidiary of Scholastic Inc. Scholastic and associated logos are trademarks and/or registered trademarks of Scholastic Inc. Klutz and associated logos are trademarks and/or registered trademarks of Klutz. The "book and box" format is a registered trademark of Klutz.

Photos copyright: Stickers: owls: Ann Precious/Shutterstock; cupcake, popsicle, ice cream cone, pretzel, cookie: ctrlaplus/Shutterstock; palm tree and sunglasses: Incomible/Fotolia; umbrella, purse, radio: Incomible/Shutterstock; fox and wolf: Marish/Shutterstock; watermelon and pineapple: mart/Shutterstock; monkey, pig, dog, mice, cat, fox: notkoo/Shutterstock; butterfly: suns07butterfly/Shutterstock; soccer ball, tennis rackets, skateboard, feather: topvectors/Fotolia. Book: 8 book paint splatters: tatiana_ti/Fotolia.

Distributed in the UK by
Scholastic UK Ltd
Westfield Road
Southam, Warwickshire
England CV47 0RA

Distributed in Canada by
Scholastic Canada Ltd
604 King Street West
Toronto, Ontario
Canada M5V 1E1

Distributed in Australia by
Scholastic Australia Ltd
PO Box 579
Gosford, NSW
Australia 2250

Distributed in Hong Kong by
Scholastic Hong Kong Ltd
Suites 2001-2, Top Glory Tower
262 Gloucester Road
Causeway Bay, Hong Kong

ISBN 978-0-545-85848-9

4 1 5 8 5 7 0 8 8 8

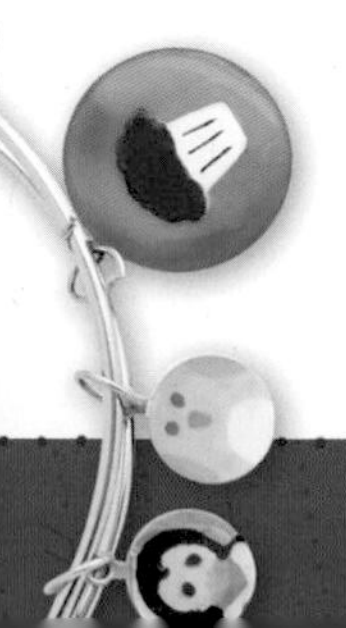

We make Klutz books using resources that have been approved by the Forest Stewardship Council™. This means the paper in this book comes exclusively from trees that have been grown and harvested responsibly.

CONTENTS

SYMBOLS

ZODIAC SIGNS

PERSONAL ICONS

Style Statements 34–37

Creative Expression 38–41

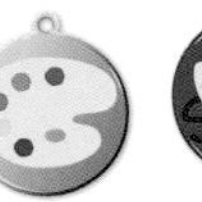

Game Day 42–45

Sweets & Treats 46–49

EMOJI

50–51

WHAT YOU GET

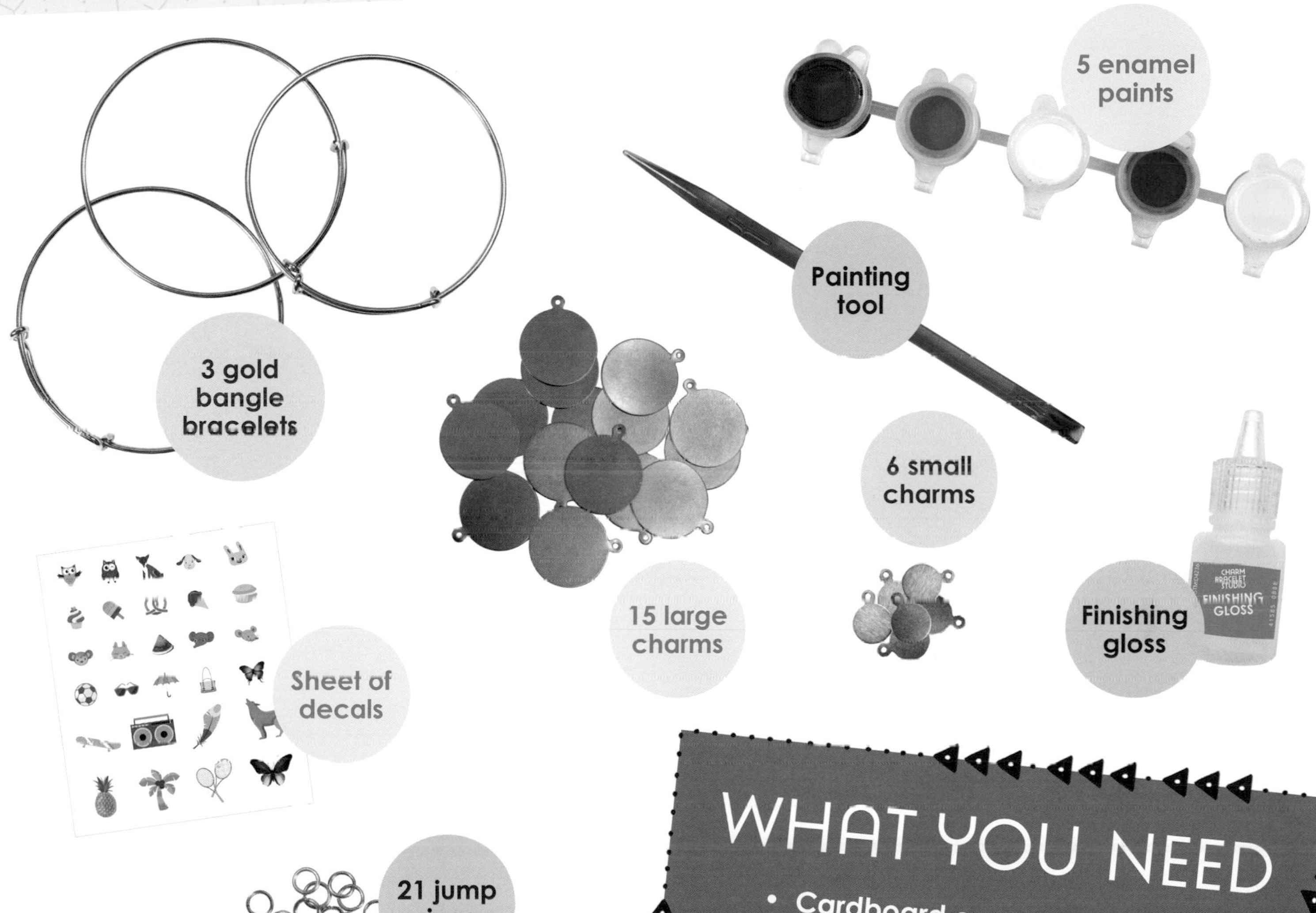

WHAT YOU NEED

- Cardboard or newspaper to protect your work surface
- Sheet of scrap paper
- Nail file
- Double-sided tape
- Water in a disposable cup (for cleaning your painting tool)
- Paper towel or disposable rag

SETTING UP YOUR STUDIO

COVER YOUR WORK SURFACE

Before you start, cover your work surface with something you won't mind splattering with paint, like cardboard or newspaper. Not that you're messy . . . but it's best to have protection in case there is a spill. Unwanted paint marks are sometimes hard to scrub out of clothes and furniture.

SET UP YOUR CHARMS

Now that your surface is protected, arrange the charms you want to paint in front of you. If you have double-sided tape handy, stick a piece of it onto the scrap paper and place the charms on top. Now the charms won't move by mistake when you do detailed work.

GATHER YOUR SUPPLIES

Collect the painting tool, paints, water, and paper towels or a rag so that they're easy to reach. Don't forget this book! Now you are ready to start making something truly charming.

PAINTING YOUR CHARMS

USING YOUR PAINTING TOOL

The painting tool has a pointy end and a flat end.

The flat end is good for painting bigger areas and solid-colored backgrounds.

The pointy end is good for adding details like dots and lines.

PRACTICE

You can practice using the painting tool on the scrap paper around your charm.

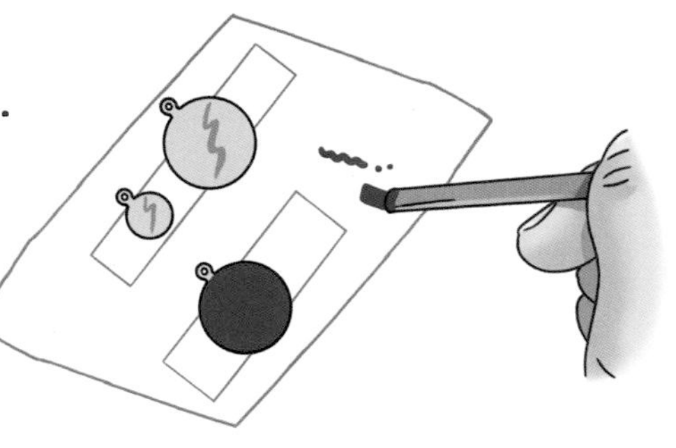

FILL

Dip the flat end of the tool into the paint. Use this end of the stick to paint a big area (like the entire face of a charm).

When you are done using the flat end of the tool, dip it into the water and wipe it clean with your paper towel or rag. If you want to paint on top of this color, you will need to let it dry completely first.

DOTS, LINES, AND SHAPES

Now dip the pointy end of the tool into the paint. If there is too much paint on the tip of the stick, wipe it off on the edge of the paint tub.

To make dots, carefully hold the tool upright above your charm. Then tap the stick on the surface quickly to make a small dot. The more paint you have on the tip of the stick, the bigger the dot will be.

To make lines and shapes, dip your tool into the paint. Then draw with your paint stick as you would with a pencil. If the line is not smooth, dip the paint stick into the paint again.

When you are done painting with this side of the stick, dip it into the water and wipe it clean with your paper towel or rag.

Remember, always let each layer of paint dry before applying the next.

MIXING COLORS

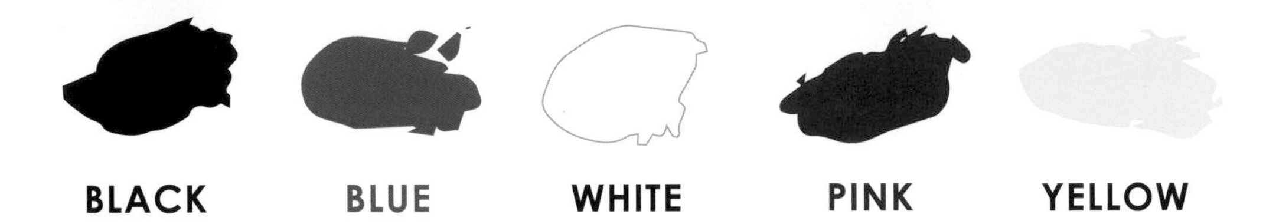

NEW COLORS

There are five colors of paint in the box attached to this book. You can mix them together to make new colors by following these recipes. Also, regular nail polish paint—the kind you get from the drugstore—works well on these charms if you want to try different colors. Just be careful to use nail polish in a ventilated area, and use nail polish remover to clean your painting tool.

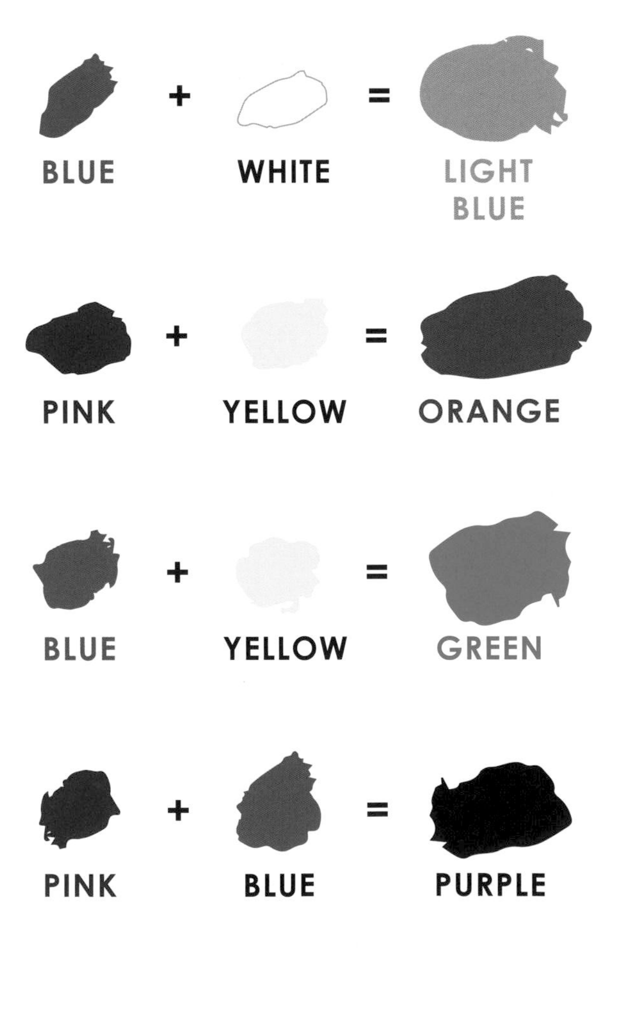

FINISHING YOUR BRACELET

FINISHING WITH GLOSS

Finishing gloss makes everything look super professional. After you paint your charms (and let them dry completely), apply the finishing gloss to make your charms shine.

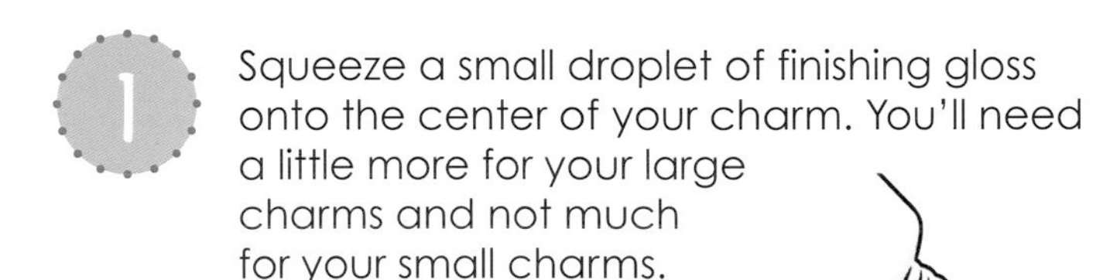

1. Squeeze a small droplet of finishing gloss onto the center of your charm. You'll need a little more for your large charms and not much for your small charms.

2. Using the nozzle of the finishing gloss bottle, slowly push the droplet of gloss out to the edges of the charm. Try not to go over the edge or cover the hole at the top of the charm.

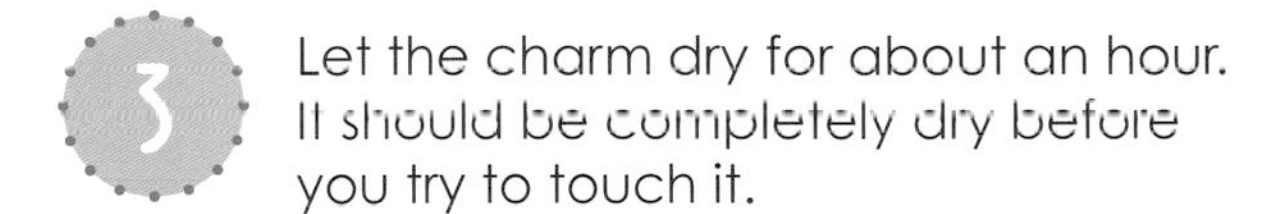

3. Let the charm dry for about an hour. It should be completely dry before you try to touch it.

4. When the gloss is dry, pull the charm off the double-sided tape. If there's excess gloss on the edges of your charm, don't worry—you can carefully remove it by filing it off with a nail file.

5. When your charm is absolutely, totally, positively dry, you can flip it over and paint another design on the back, or leave it gold.

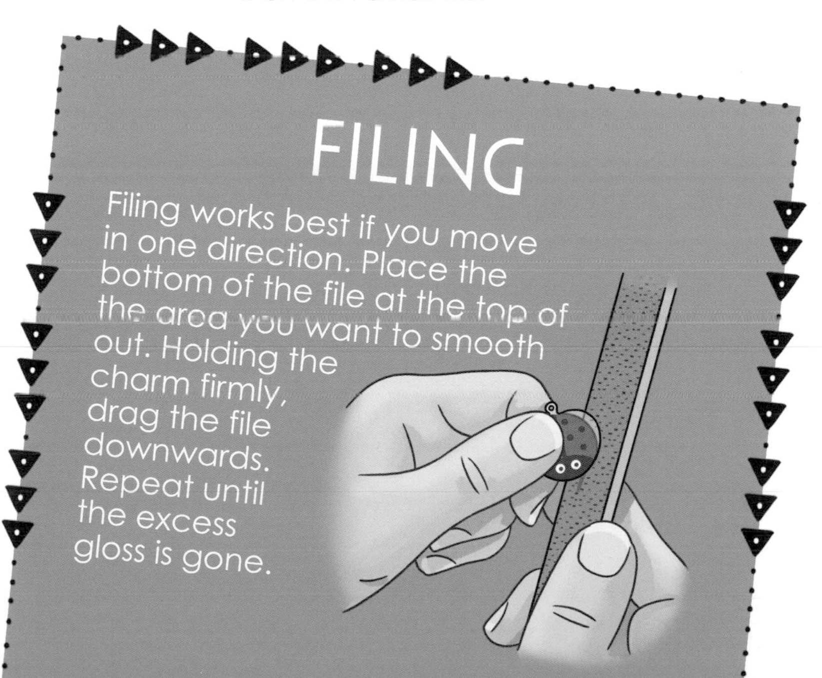

ADDING JUMP RINGS

When your charm is glazed and dry, you can attach it to a bangle bracelet.

Hold the jump ring so that the split of the ring faces up toward the ceiling. Hold the sides of the ring with the thumb and pointer finger of each hand.

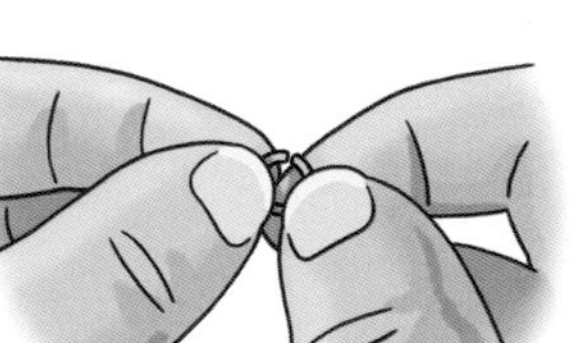

Slowly twist open the ring by moving your right hand backward and your left hand forward. You only need to open the ring enough to fit the charm and bangle through.

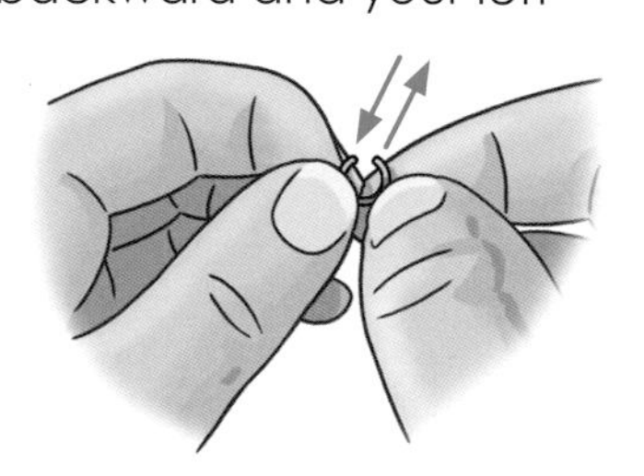

Loop the jump ring through the hole in the charm, then place the bangle through the center of the open jump ring.

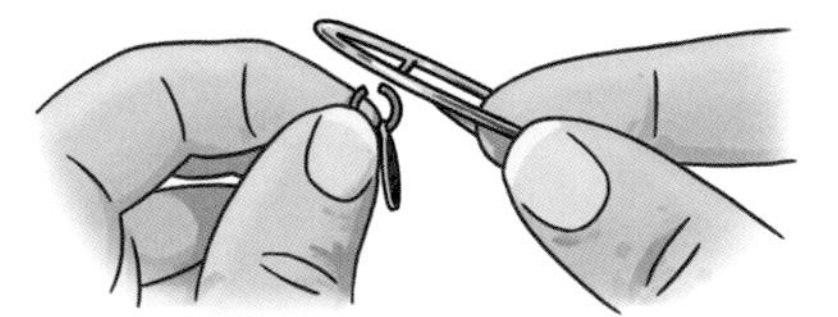

Twist the jump ring back into a closed position by bringing your right hand forward and your left hand backward. The closer the ends are together, the more secure your charm will be on the bracelet.

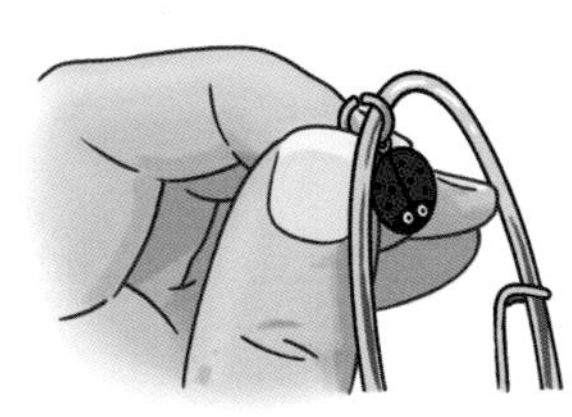

Add a very small drop of gloss to the jump ring where the ends meet to prevent the charm from falling off your bracelet. Let the gloss dry.

You might want to ask an adult for help with this step because it gets a bit tricky. For additional help, use needle-nose pliers to grab the sides of the ring.

PERSONALIZATION

COMBINING CHARMS

Mix, match, and make charms to fit your own personality (or someone else who's super awesome). With so many designs and meanings to choose from, each charm combo is unique . . . and made by you!

OTHER WAYS TO WEAR

Each charm is meant to be personalized for the wearer's interests, but they don't all have to dangle from a bangle bracelet. Here are some alternative ideas:

- Add one charm or many charms to a chain to make a necklace or bracelet.
- Use embroidery floss to knot charms into a friendship bracelet or simple braid.
- Attach charms to earring hooks.
- Add a charm to a lobster clasp and attach it to a zipper on your sweatshirt or backpack.
- Fasten charms to a key chain for a little luck wherever you go.

GOOD KARMA

These charms will bring good fortune and positive thinking when you wear them.

YIN-YANG

This ancient Eastern symbol represents the balance of two opposite forces.

1 2 3

LOTUS FLOWER

Blooming on the water's surface, with roots deep below, the lotus flower symbolizes life, purity, and the rising sun.

1 2 3 4

OM

The sound of the om (pronounced: OH-mm), a Hindu syllable, is the essence of the universe in harmony.

1 2 3

FEATHER

A weightless reminder to be hopeful, the feather also represents the search for truth.

ANKH

Gods and pharaohs were often shown holding this symbol, an ancient Egyptian hieroglyph that means "life."

EVIL EYE

This eastern Mediterranean charm was created for protection.

FOUR-LEAF CLOVER

Only one out of 10,000 clover plants has four leaflets, so finding one is a sign of good luck.

HORSESHOE

This shape has stood for good fortune since the Middle Ages. Luck is caught in the bend, and runs out through the ends.

ANCHOR

In rough waters,
a heavy anchor can
keep you grounded
and centered.

1	2	3	4

KEY

Even the toughest of
puzzles can be unlocked
if you have the right key. It
represents both ingenuity
and intrigue.

1	2	3	4

PEACE SIGN

Made popular by the hippies of the 1960s, this sign represents peace for all humankind.

1 2 3

FLOWER POWER

Flowers signify growth, renewal, and grace against adversity.

1 2

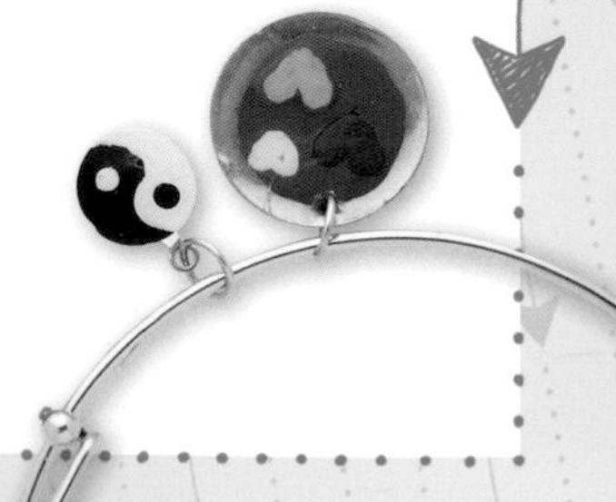

STARBURST

The stars guide us when we've lost our way. They symbolize the wonder of the universe and a light shining amid vast darkness.

SHOOTING STAR

The ancient Greeks believed that shooting stars appear when the gods look down at Earth. Shooting stars stand for protection and for wishes you hope will come true.

HEART

Many ancient cultures believed the heart, not the brain, was physically responsible for thoughts and emotions. The heart remains a symbol for love and devotion.

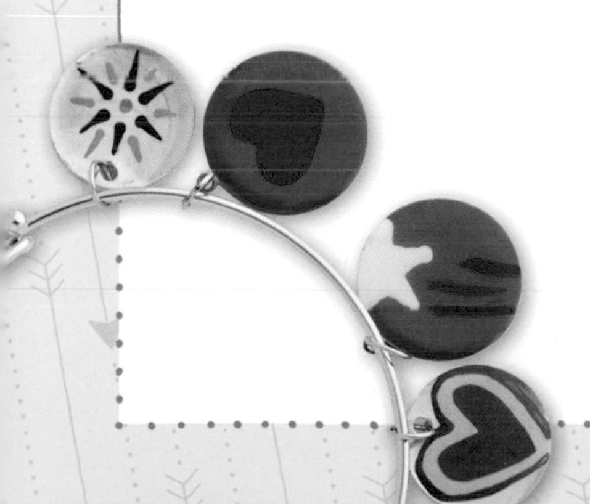

SPIRIT ANIMALS

Some special characteristics are represented in the wild. Find your animal inspiration!

BEE

This insect represents hard work for the good of the community, with the reward of sweet honey.

 2 3

BUTTERFLY

The caterpillar's transformation into a butterfly represents new beginnings.

 2 3 4

LADYBUG

Ladybugs protect plants from other insects and are a sign of safety, fearlessness, and promise of renewal.

 2  

DRAGONFLY

Older than the dinosaurs, dragonflies embody strength and resilience.

 2 

OWL

Since an owl's unique eyes can see clearly in the dark, its image is known to represent wisdom.

1

2

3

4

SWAN

These birds choose just one partner to be with for life, which is why swans represent devoted love.

1

2

3

4

PENGUIN

With a strong family bond that always brings them home, penguins have the courage and freedom to venture far and wide.

1

2

3

4

FROG

An amphibian that's just as comfortable in water as on land, the frog stands for adaptability.

2

3

4

TURTLE

They never panic or hurry, because turtles carry everything they need with them at all times: strong protection outside, and deep tranquility inside.

2

CHICK

If you could concentrate sunshine into a tiny, huggable ball, it would look like a baby chick—a symbol of springtime and new life.

1

2

3

COW

1 2  3 4

Civilization owes a huge debt to cows. They're considered sacred in the Hindu religion, representing serenity and Mother Earth.

CAT

1 2 3 4

Felines are known for their dual personalities: One moment they can be fiercely independent, and the next they're creatures of pure empathy with a belly full of purrs.

DOG

1 2 3

Commonly known as humankind's best friend, dogs represent loyalty.

LION

This big cat is the king of the jungle because of its strength and beauty. The lion symbolizes royalty and bravery.

BEAR

With their enormous stature, bears represent confidence and strength. They stand for leadership and taking action against adversity.

1

2

3

MOTHER NATURE

Wear these charms to harness the power of our gorgeous planet Earth.

MOUNTAINS

Mountains represent adventure, and the challenge of overcoming big obstacles.

WAVE

Waves have a range of meanings—from the soothing rhythm of the sea, to the ups and downs of life.

TREE

Trees give us so much: shade, oxygen, fruit, and good climbing! This image shows a respect for nature and its gifts.

PALM TREE

These trees only survive in tropical, warm weather. They often represent relaxation.

RAIN CLOUD

Here's a reminder that sometimes when it rains, you should let it be.

RAINBOW

This natural wonder of color and light is a symbol of peace, hope, and embracing diversity.

SUN

The sun is the source of all life and warmth. Use this symbol to express your own bright, cheery attitude.

WINTER SNOWFLAKE

The winter brings joyous anticipation of snow and holidays.

1 

2 

3 

FALL LEAF

The colorful leaves of fall represent change and the cycle of seasons.

1 

2 

3 

SPRING TULIPS

Tulips appear in many beautiful colors, when the cold months are over and the promise of spring is in the air.

1 

2 

3 

SUMMER SUNFLOWER

A sunflower turns its face to follow the summer sun as it moves across the sky.

1 

2 

3 

ZODIAC SIGNS

Astrological symbols are said to carry traits for those born under a particular star sign.

ARIES

March 21–April 19
creative, adaptable, insightful

TAURUS

April 20–May 20
strong, determined, purposeful

GEMINI

May 21–June 20
flexible, balanced, adaptable

CANCER

June 21–July 22
traditional, loyal, sympathetic

LEO

July 23–August 22
brave, intuitive, headstrong

VIRGO

August 23–September 22
thoughtful, practical, analytical

LIBRA

September 23–October 22
balanced, just, stable

SCORPIO

October 23–November 22
bold, confident, focused

SAGITTARIUS

November 23–December 21
focused, loyal, philosophical

CAPRICORN

December 22–January 19
intelligent, practical, stable

AQUARIUS

January 20–February 19
honest, loyal, intelligent

PISCES

February 20–March 20
honest, unselfish, trustworthy

XIX
THE SUN.
JUSTICE.

STYLE STATEMENTS

Whether your fashion sense is down-to-earth, edgy, or classy, you decide what you like.

BOOM BOX

1 2 3 4

SUNGLASSES

1 2 3

HEADPHONES

1 2 3

COWBOY BOOT

SNEAKER

1 2 3 4

SWIMSUIT

1 2 3

BEACH BALL

HIGH HEEL

CREATIVE EXPRESSION

Creativity drives new ideas and abilities. How do you express yourself?

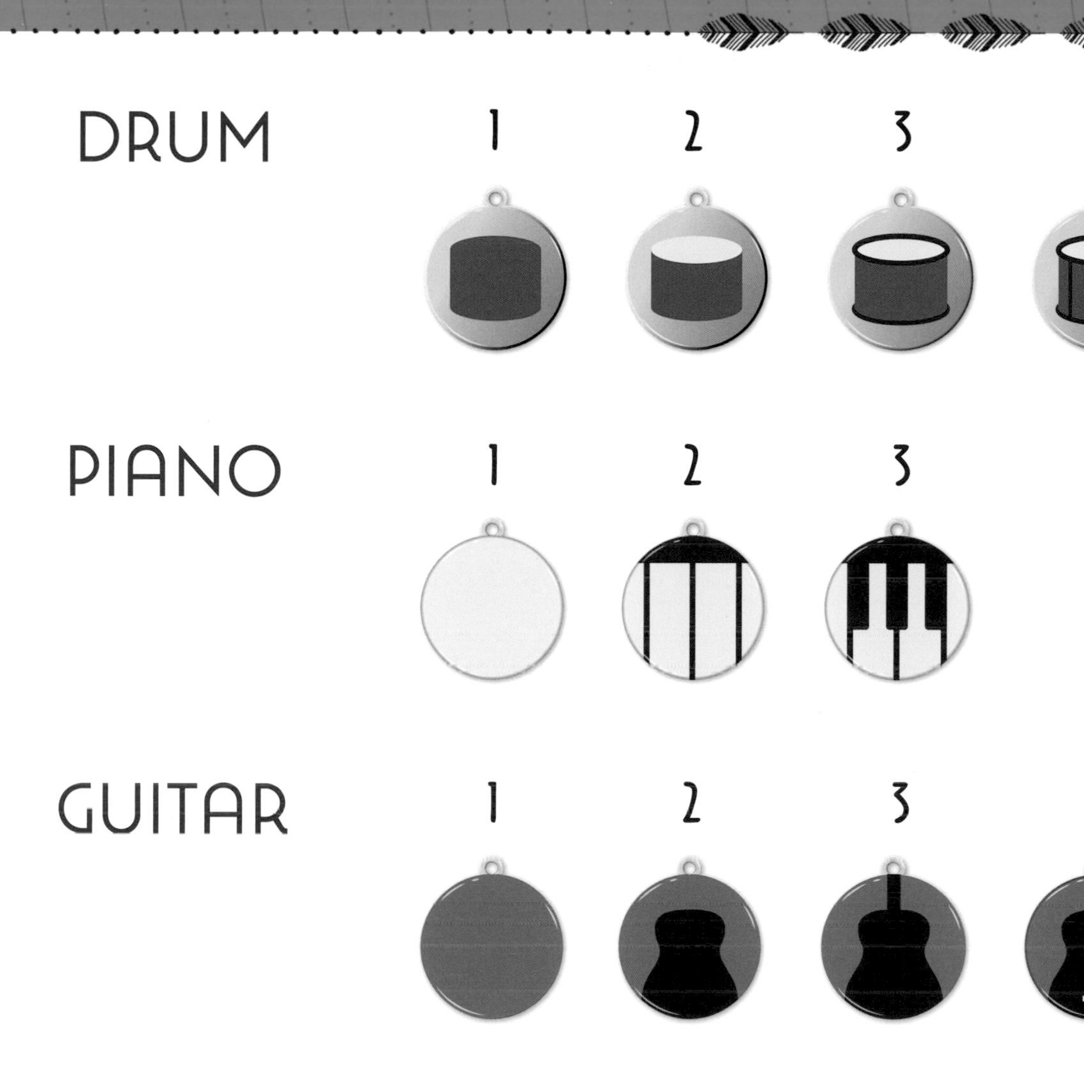

MUSIC NOTES

GAMING

1 

2 

3 

READING & WRITING

1 

2 

3 

4 

PAINTING

1 

2 

DRAMA

1 2 3 4

PHOTOGRAPHY

1 2 3

GAME DAY

It doesn't matter if you like to win or you just like to move. Exercise is good for the body and the mind.

CHEERLEADING

1 2 3

SWIMMING

1 2 3

TRACK & FIELD

1 2 3 4

HOCKEY

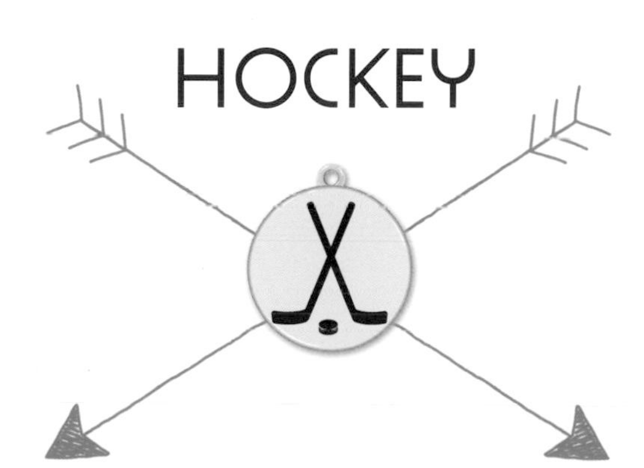

ICE-SKATING

1 2 3 4

SAILING

1 2 3

BALLET

1 2 3 4

TENNIS

SOCCER

BASEBALL

FOOTBALL

BASKETBALL

VOLLEYBALL

SWEETS & TREATS

Sometimes just the thought of something delicious makes you feel good. Treat yourself!

WATERMELON

1 | 2 | 3 | 4

STRAWBERRY

1 | 2 | 3

GRAPES

1 | 2 | 3 | 4

APPLE

GUMBALL MACHINE

1	2	3

ICE CREAM

1	2	3

CUPCAKE

1	2	3	4

DOUGHNUT

1	2	3

FRIES

1 2 3

HAMBURGER

1 2 3

LOLLIPOPS

EMOJI

The word *emoji* is a mash-up of the Japanese words for "picture" and "letter."

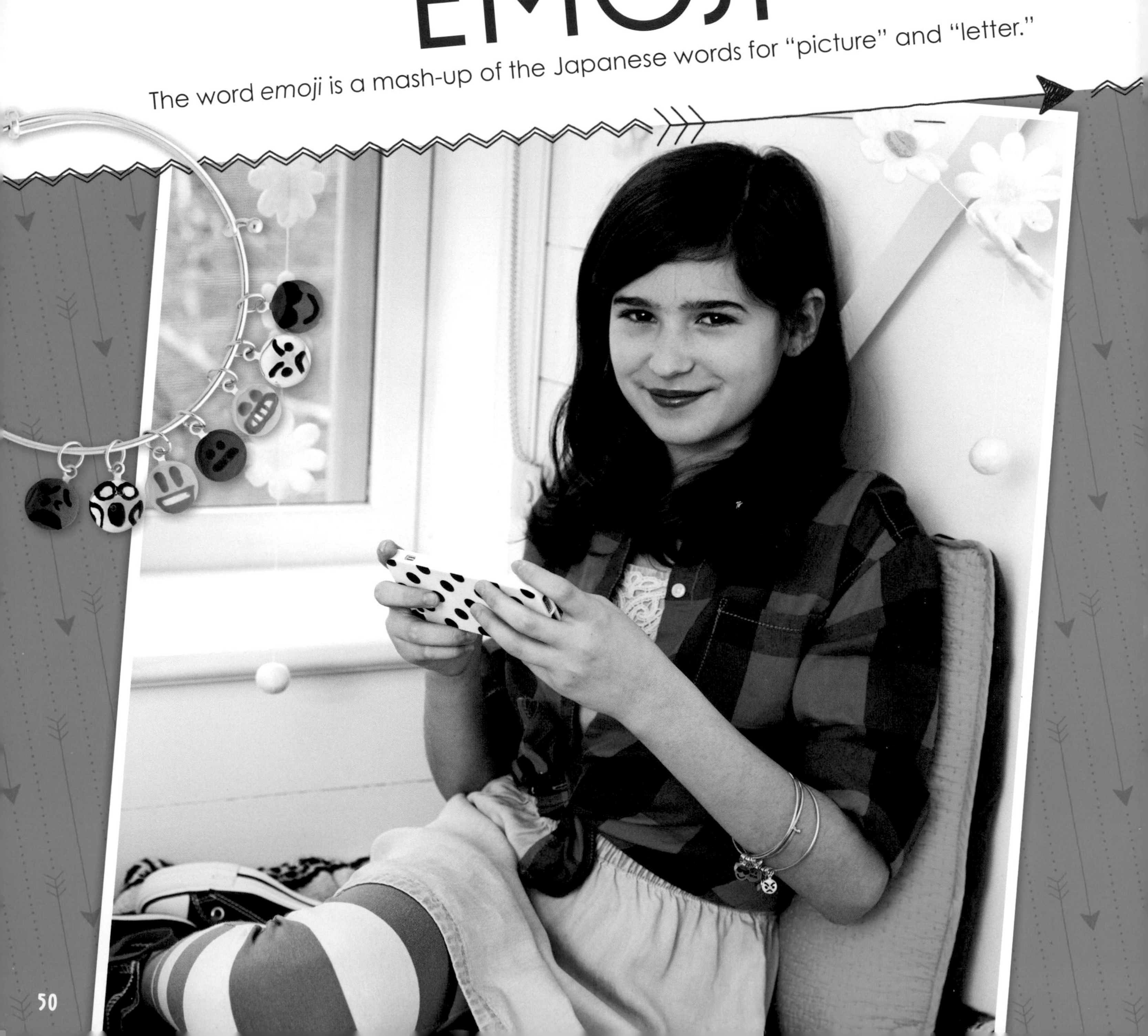

HAPPY

MEH

SAD

PSYCHED

WINK

SURPRISED

COOL

WORRIED

ANGRY

CREDITS

Blue Aura (guiding light): Hannah Rogge
Butterfly (new beginnings): Dan Letchworth
Starburst (clarity through illustration): Jim Kopp
Bee (dedicated work on illustration): Kyle Hilton
Anchor (grounded and centered design): Sarah Baker
Key (ingenuity and intrigue through photography): Lucy Schaeffer
Rainbow (styling with colors and light): Martha Bernabe
Icons: Sophia, Hannah, Indira, Shannon, Bella, Piper, and Helena
Shooting Star (making wishes come true): Kelly Shaffer
Paint Palettes (flexing artistic skills): Katie Benezra, Caitlin Harpin, and Netta Rabin
Feathers (searching for truth): F. S. Kim and Barrie Zipkin
Turtle (packing all that is needed): Owen Keating
Om (bringing harmony): Stacy Lellos